Published By Adam Gilbin

@ Mike Dean

Paleo Diet: Simple to Follow Guide a

Comprehensive Guide to Combining Paleo Diets

for Special Populations

All Right RESERVED

ISBN 978-87-94477-66-6

TABLE OF CONTENTS

Westernstyle Breakfast Omelet 1

Applesauce Pancakes 3

Slow Cooker Pork Loin 4

Turkey Meatballs 7

Tikka Masala 10

Chicken Broth 14

Beef Broth 16

Paleo Nachos 19

Grilled Vegetable Salad 22

Paleo Mojito 25

Chicken "Tacos" 27

Coconut Banana Pancakes 29

Nutty Kale And Beef Salad With Tangerine Lime Dressing
.... 31

Cauliflower Crust Pizza 33

Energy Bars 36

Egg Rolls 38

Citrus & Napa Cabbage Salad	41
Easy Roasted Zucchini	43
Gomen	44
Instant Pot Butter Chicken	45
Veggiepacked Turkey Meatloaf	49
Golden Glow Soup	52
Wholewheat Flatbreads With Beans & Poached Egg	54
Smoky Mushroom & Potato Hash With Oaty Thins	57
Pineapplecashew Soup	60
Green Peas – Carrot Soup	62
Onion Soup	65
Aip Lamb And Root Vegetable	67
Aip Chicken And Vegetable Stew	69
Aip Beef And Root Vegetable Stew	71
Zucchini Fritters With Avocado Dipping Sauce	72
Turkey And Sweet Potato Chili	75
Roasted Garlic And Herb Pork Tenderloin	76
Salmon Veggie Bowls With Sesame Seeds	78

Tilapia Veracruz 80

Shrimp And Sausage Skillet 82

Sweet Potato Hash Browns 85

Turkey Sausage Breakfast 87

Turkey, Bacon Lettuce Wraps With Basil And Mayonnaise 89

Chop & Drop Roasted Veggies & Sausage 92

Portobello Burgers 95

Chicken And Sweet Potato Skillet 98

Sesame Steak And Vegetable Stir Fry 100

Baked Salmon With Lemon And Pecan Green Beans ... 102

Butter Chicken 104

Slow Cooker Ham 107

Pumpkin Slow Cooker Coconut Curry 108

Vegetable Broth 110

Curry Paste 111

Frittata 114

No Flour No Sugar Paleo Brownie 116

Dark Chocolate Mousse 118

Quick And Easy Garlic Shrimp 121

Lamb And Cilantro Stir Fry.. 123

Beef Stirfry.. 124

Cauliflower Rice.. 127

Stirfry... 129

Creamy Dill Garlic Salmon 132

Bang Bang Shrimp 134

Homemade Cilantro Lime Ranch Dressing 135

Grilled Lemonherb Chicken 137

Maplechili Roasted Butternut Squash.......................... 140

Westernstyle Breakfast Omelet

Ingredients:

- 2 green bell pepper, diced

- 1 teaspoon extra virgin olive oil

- 1/4 teaspoon unrefined sea salt

- 4 ounces mushrooms

- 4 large eggs

- 1/4 pound ham, cooked and diced

- 2 medium tomato diced

- 2 half medium yellow onion, diced

- Black pepper to taste

Directions:

1. Crack the eggs into a small bowl. Wash and dice the vegetables. Heat a nonstick skillet on medium, and add the oil.
2. Pour half of the beaten eggs into the skillet. When your eggs are partially set, scrape the edges so that the uncooked eggs can spread to the surface.
3. Add half of the vegetables and ham to half the omelette.
4. Cook until eggs are almost set. With a spatula, fold the empty half over the top of the ham and vegetables.
5. Cook for 3 min longer. Repeat this process with the remaining Ingredients: to make the second omelet. Makes 3 servings.

Applesauce Pancakes

Ingredients:

- 2 tablespoons coconut flour

- 4 eggs

- 1/2 teaspoon nutmeg

- 1/2 teaspoon unrefined sea salt

- 1/2 cup water

- 2 cups almond flour

- 2 tablespoons coconut oil

- 1 cup unsweetened applesauce

- 1 cup fresh raspberries, blueberries

Directions:

1. Mix together the almond flour, applesauce, coconut flour, eggs, water, nutmeg, and sea salt into a bowl.
2. Mix these well, as the batter will be thick. In a nonstick skillet, heat on medium low and add the coconut oil.
3. Place 1/2 cup batter into the pan. Flip the pancakes when the bubbles start appearing.
4. Cook for a few minutes more, and add more oil.
5. Repeat this process with the remaining batter. Top the pancakes with the fresh berries. Makes 4 servings.

Slow Cooker Pork Loin

Ingredients:

- 1 tart apple, peeled and diced

- 1 small onion, chopped

- 1 clove garlic, minced

- 1/4 cup raisins

- 1/4 cup flaked coconut

- 2 pounds b2 less pork loin, cut into 1inch cubes

- 2 tablespoons cold water

- 1/2 cup orange juice

- 1 tablespoon curry powder

- 1 teaspoon chicken bouillon granules

- 1/2 teaspoon ground ginger

- 1/4 teaspoon ground cinnamon

- 1/2 teaspoon salt

Directions:

1. Combine orange juice, curry powder, chicken bouillon, ginger, cinnamon, and salt in a slow cooker.
2. Stir in the apple, onion, garlic, raisins, and coconut. Place pork cubes in the sauce.
3. Whisk together the water and potato starch in a small bowl until there are no lumps; stir into slow cooker.
4. Cover; cook on Low until pork is very tender, 5 to 6 hours.

Turkey Meatballs

Ingredients:

- 1/2 tsp onion powder

- 1/2 tsp garlic powder

- 1 tsp salt

- 1/2 cup almond meal

- 1 egg, beaten

- 24 oz San Marzano crushed tomatoes

- 1/2 large onion, quartered

- 2 cloves garlic, crushed

- 1 lb ground turkey

- 1 lb turkey sausage (ground or in casing)

- 1 tsp basil

- 1/2 tsp oregano

- 1/2 tsp rosemary

- 1/2 tsp thyme

- 2 tbsp red wine vinegar

Directions:
1. Begin by heating a large skillet to medium high.
2. In a large bowl, mix together both ground turkey and sausage until well blended.
3. In a separate small bowl, mix together basil, oregano, rosemary, garlic powder, onion powder, salt, and almond meal. Add mixture to the meat.
4. With your hands, mix together the spices and meat until well incorporated. Add in beaten egg and continue to mix well.

5. Form meat mixture into large meatballs (about 1.52 inches in diameter).
6. Grease your skillet, and add meatballs. Cook each meatball about 1 minute per side until the meat is browned (but not cooked through). Add meatballs to slow cooker.
7. Top meatballs with tomatoes, onion, garlic, and vinegar.
8. Cook on low for 56 hours.
9. Serve plain with fresh basil, or with spaghetti squash.

Tikka Masala

Ingredients:

- 1/2 large white or yellow onion, thinly sliced

- 1 TBSP + 2 tsp garam masala

- 1 tsp ground coriander

- 1 tsp ground cumin

- 1/2 tsp kosher salt (less for finer grain)

- 1/4 tsp red chili flakes

- 1 TBSP coconut palm suga

- 2 TBSP butter or coconut oil

- 2 pounds chicken thighs, b2 in and skinon.

- 1 cup fullfat canned coconut milk

- 2 cups organic crushed tomatoes

- 1 TBSP fresh ginger root, minced

- 3 cloves garlic, minced

- Optional: cilantro for garnish

Directions:

1. Prep and clean the chicken thighs (remove excess fat and skin), place in a bowl and coat in 1 tablespoon of garam masala.
2. Heat a pan to mediumhigh and melt a couple tablespoons of coconut oil.
3. Sear the chicken thighs, starting with the skinside down. We just need a quick sear on both sides, then place in the slow cooker.
4. Thinly slice half an onion and lay on top of the chicken thighs.
5. In a sauce pan, melt the 2 tablespoons of butter or ghee with the minced ginger root and garlic on medium heat.
6. When the garlic and ginger sizzles, add the coconut milk and crushed tomatoes.
7. The spices go next — 2 teaspoons of garam masala, the coriander, cumin, salt, red chili flakes and coconut palm sugar.

8. Simmer for just a few minutes, until the spices are well mixed and the sauce starts bubble.
9. Pour the sauce over the onions and chicken thighs already waiting in the slow cooker.
10. Cover and set the slow cooker to low. Cook for 3 to 4 hours.

Chicken Broth

Ingredients:

- 1 carrot

- 8 black peppercorns

- 2 sprigs fresh thyme

- 2 sprigs fresh parsley

- 4 lbs. fresh chicken (wings, necks, backs, legs, b2 s)

- 2 peeled onions or 1 cup chopped leeks

- 2 celery stalks

- 1 tsp. salt

Directions:

1. Put cold water in a stock pot and add chicken. Bring just to a boil. Skim any foam from the surface.
2. Add other Ingredients:, return just to a boil, and reduce heat to a slow simmer. Simmer for 2 hours.
3. Let cool to warm room temperature and strain. Keep chilled and use or freeze broth within a few days. Before using, defrost and boil.

Beef Broth

Ingredients:

- 12 large carrots, cut into 12 inch segments

- 1 celery rib, cut into 1 inch segments

- 23 cloves of garlic, unpeeled

- Handful of parsley, stems and leaves

- 12 bay leaves

- 45 pounds beef b2 s and few veal b2 s

- 1 pound of stew meat (chuck or flank steak) cut into 2inch chunks

- olive oil or avocado oil

- 12 medium onions, peeled and quartered

- 10 peppercorns

Directions:

1. Heat oven to 375°F. Rub olive oil over the stew meat pieces, carrots, and onions. Place stew meat or beef scraps, stock b2 s, carrots and onions in a large roasting pan. Roast in oven for about 45 minutes, turning everything halfway through the cooking.
2. Place everything from the oven in a large stock pot. Pour some boiling water in the oven pan and scrape up all of the browned bits and pour all in the stock pot.
3. Add parsley, celery, garlic, bay leaves, and peppercorns to the pot. Fill the pot with cold water, to 1 inch over the top of the b2 s. Bring the stock pot to a regular simmer and then reduce the heat to low, so it just barely simmers. Cover the pot loosely and let simmer low and slow for 34 hours.

4. Scoop away the fat and any scum that rises to the surface once in a while.
5. After cooking, remove the b2 s and vegetables from the pot. Strain the broth. Let cool to room temperature and then put in the refrigerator.
6. The fat will solidify once the broth has chilled. Discard the fat (or reuse it) and pour the broth into a jar and freeze it.

Paleo Nachos

Ingredients:

- Fresh cilantro, finely chopped 2
- Lime juice 2 tbsp.
- Guacamole 2 cups
- Medium tomatoes, diced and seeded 2
- Green onions, finely chopped – 2 tbsp.

Chips

- Large sweet potatoes 3
- Melted coconut oil 3 tbsp.
- Salt 1 tsp

Meat topping

- Ground beef 1lb.

- Cloves garlic, minced 2
- Smoked paprika 1/2
- Medium onion, finely diced 1
- Coconut oil – 1 tbsp.
- Green chili, diced 1
- Ground cumin – ½ tsp
- Tomato paste 1 tbsp.
- Canned diced tomatoes 12 oz.
- Salt to taste
- Pepper ½ tsp (optional)

Directions:

1. **Sweet potato chips**: Preheat the oven to 375°F. Peel the potatoes and slice them very thinly.
2. Next mix them with the coconut oil and salt and place them on a baking sheet and in the oven for 10 minutes.
3. Flip the chips and bake for another 10 minutes. Just keep a watch in the last few minutes and remove chips as they start browning.
4. **Meat Topping:** In a skillet heat the oil and sauté the onion and chili for 34 minutes, stirring continuously so as to not burn the onions. Once they are nicely d2 , add the beef and cook for another 5 minutes.
5. This is followed by adding the garlic, tomatoes, tomato paste and the rest of the spices.
6. Mix it well and bring the mixture to a boil and then simmer on medium flame before cooking

it covered for 2025 minutes. Remember to stir frequently.

7. Once the beef mixture is d2 , add the chopped tomatoes and lime juice and garnish with cilantro. Check if salt is okay and bring down from the flame.
8. Now is the best part; assembly. Arrange the sweet potato chips on a platter and cover it with the beef mixture.
9. Put the guacamole on the top of the mixture and garnish with the green onions.

Grilled Vegetable Salad

Ingredients:

- Red onion, thinly sliced 1

- Asparagus ends trimmed1 lb.

- Extra virgin olive oil, for drizzling
- Medium zucchini 3
- Medium yellow squash 1
- Red bell pepper 1
- Yellow bell pepper 1

For the sauce

- 1/4 cup paleo mayonnaise 1/4 cup
- Juice of 1 lime
- Cloves garlic, crushed 2
- Cumin 1 tsp
- Salt & pepper, to taste

Directions:

1. Slice the vegetable to any shape of your choice and drizzle salt and pepper on top of the slices.
2. Preheat the grill and place the vegetables on it. Coat the veggies lightly with oil. You have to grill for 1012 minutes before serving.
3. In another bowl whisk the Ingredients: of the sauce together and season with cumin.
4. Serve the veggies along with the sauce or just gently mix the sauce with the grilled veggies.
5. It makes a nice accompaniment to the soup.

Paleo Mojito

Ingredients:

- Juice of 1 lime
- Mint sprigs 2
- Ice cubes 10
- Strawberries 10
- H2 y 1 tbsp.
- Sparkling water

Directions:

1. Roughly blend the strawberries and the mint springs. Add lime juice and h2 y to the mixture and mix it well.
2. Place the ice cubes and the mixture in a glass and top it with sparkling water.

3. Paleo mojito is ready to be sipped and enjoyed.

Chicken "Tacos"

Ingredients:

- 12 romaine lettuce leaves

- 3 mediumsized tomatoes (or 2 large tomatoes)

- 2 small avocadoes (or 1 large avocado)

- 1 onion

- 1 tbsp olive oil (or preferred oil)

- 6 chicken breasts or thighs

- 1 tsp garlic powder

- 1/2 tsp onion powder

- 1/2 tsp sea salt

- 1/2 cup chicken broth

Directions:

1. Add the garlic powder, onions powder, sea salt, and chicken broth to a sauce pan. Stir to combine and heat on medium heat.
2. Cut the chicken into small, bitesized chunks and add to the sauce pan. Bring to a simmer, then turn the heat down to low. Cook until the chicken is d2 .
3. While the chicken is cooking, dice the tomatoes, avocadoes, and onion. Mix together in a bowl and drizzle olive oil. Salt to taste.
4. Remove the chicken from the pan once cooked. Let cool.
5. Using the lettuce leaves as a "taco" shell, fill with chicken. Top each taco with the tomato mixture and serve.

Coconut Banana Pancakes

Ingredients:

- 1/4 cup coconut milk

- 1/4 cup coconut flour, sifted

- 1/4 tsp cream of tartar

- 1/8 tsp baking soda

- 2 tbsp coconut oil

- 1 tbsp raw h2 y

- 3 eggs

- 1 small banana, mashed

- Pinch of sea salt

Directions:

1. Combine the coconut oil and h2 y in a bowl and mix until creamy.
2. Add the eggs 2 at a time, mixing after each 2 .
3. Add coconut milk and coconut flour. Mix until smooth.
4. Add the mashed banana, cream of tartar, baking soda, and salt. Mix until smooth.
5. Pour small amounts of batter into a pan on medium heat. Flip once when the bottom is a light brown and not sticking to the pan. Serve immediately.

Nutty Kale And Beef Salad With Tangerine Lime Dressing

Ingredients:

- 2 tbsp olive oil

- 2 tsp balsamic vinegar

- 1 tsp sea salt

- Juice of half a tangerine

- 1 lb. sirloin steak, cut into thin strips

- 1 large bunch of kale

- 1/4 cup almonds

- 1/4 cup walnuts

- Juice of half a lime

Directions:

1. Lightly salt the steak and cook over mediumhigh heat in a pan or a skillet. Set aside.
2. In a small bowl, whisk together the olive oil, balsamic vinegar, sea salt, tangerine juice, and lime juice. Add more sea salt to taste.
3. Chop the kale and add to a large bowl. Pour the dressing into the bowl and gently massage the kale with your hands until kale is wilted.
4. Chop the almonds and walnuts. Toss into the bowl.
5. Add the steak and lightly d2 . Refrigerate until ready to serve.

Cauliflower Crust Pizza

Ingredients:

- 2 garlic cloves (minced)

- 1 cup of almond flour

- 2 tablespoons of flax meal

- 1½ teaspoons of baking powder

- ¼ cup of garbanzo bean flour

- 2 tablespoons of cornmeal

- ½ a head of large a cauliflower (cut into florets, about 3 cups)

- 1 tablespoon of olive oil

- ¼ onion (chopped)

- nonstick cooking spray

Directions:

1. Preheat the oven to 375 degrees. Place a piece of parchment paper on a baking sheet and spray it lightly down with the spray.
2. Place the cauliflower florets into a food processor. Keep processing the cauliflower until it is close to the same consistency of rice.
3. Heat the olive oil in a large skillet and saute the onion, garlic, and processed cauliflower until it is softened. Set to the side to cool.
4. In a large bowl, combine the almond flour, flax meal, cornmeal, garbanzo bean flour, and the cauliflower mixture. Mix together with your hands until a dough is formed.
5. Flatten out the dough onto the baking sheet into the shape of a pizza. If you are only making 2 pizza, then the remaining dough can be put in the refrigerator wrapped up for several days.

6. Bake the crust for 20 minutes or until the edges start to become crisp. Remove from the oven and spread out a thin layer of sauce and add the toppings you desire.
7. Bake in the oven for another 15 minutes. Best if served hot right out of the oven.

Energy Bars

Ingredients:

- 12 or 14 Medjool dates (depitted)

- 1/2 of a dark chocolate bar

- 1 cup of whole natural almonds

- 1/4 cup of raw pumpkin seeds

Directions:

1. In a food processor, process the almonds until they are in small bits but not all the way to a paste. Place in a small mixing bowl. Do the same thing with the dark chocolate to have a nut/chocolate mixture.
2. Process the dates until they are completely smooth. Add to the mixing bowl.
3. Add in the pumpkin seeds whole. Mix all the Ingredients: together.

4. Line a 9x9 pan with parchment paper or a plastic wrap. Place and spread the mixture into the pan firmly by hand.
5. Cut into bars.

Egg Rolls

Ingredients:

For the wrappers:

- 1/4 cup of avocado oil (will use additional for frying)

- 1/2 teaspoon of sea salt

- 3 cups of yuca root (peeled, coarsely chopped, and boiled, 20 minutes to boil)

For the filling:

- 3 tablespoons of coconut aminos

- 1 cup of carrots (diced and shredded)

- 2 cups of cabbage (diced and shredded)

- 1 lb. ground pork

- 1 teaspoon of ground ginger

- 1 teaspoon of garlic sea salt blend

For the Dipping Sauce:

- 2 tablespoons of coconut aminos

- 1 ½ teaspoons coconut palm sugar

- 1/2 teaspoon of apple cider vinegar

- 1/4 teaspoon of Sriracha

- 1/4 teaspoon of hot mustard

Directions:

1. Preheat oven to 350 degrees
2. Drain and blend fully boiled yucca in a blender. Pour in avocado oil until dough is formed. Empty mixture onto parchment paper and allow to cool.
3. While the dough is cooling, brown the pork in a skillet and mix with the garlic salt, aminos, and ginger.

4. Add in the carrots and cabbage once the pork is no longer pink. Continue to cook until the pork is thoroughly cooked through and the vegetables are softened. Remove from heat.
5. Take handfuls of the cooled dough and flatten them into a tortilla on a parchment paper lined baking sheet. Square off the edges with your fingers.
6. Repeat until the baking sheet is full and bake for 10 minutes. Repeat until all the wrappers are made
7. Once the wrappers are cool, take a tablespoon of the meat mixture and place in the center. Roll together and tuck in the edges. Repeat until all the wrappers are filled. Fry in a skillet with avocado oil until all sides are brown.
8. To make the dipping sauce, simply combine all the Ingredients: in a small bowl.

Citrus & Napa Cabbage Salad

Ingredients:

- 3 cups shredded napa cabbage

- ½ cup coarsely chopped fresh cilantro

- ½ cup fried shallots (see Tips)

- 3 tbsps. fried garlic (see Tips)

- 2 large grapefruit, preferably Ruby Red

- 2 tbsps. fried shallot oil (see Tips) or canola oil

- 1 tbsp. lime juice

- 2 tsps. fish sauce (see Tips)

- ¼ jalapeño or serrano chile, seeded and minced

Directions:

1. Cut the ends of the grapefruit and use a sharp knife to remove the white pith and peel.
2. Cut the grapefruit segments from its surrounding membranes and cut them into bitesize pieces. Discard the seeds.
3. In a large bowl, combine the fish sauce, oil, and lime juice. Stir in grapefruit, shallots, cabbage, garlic, cilantro, and jalapeño (or serrano). Mix thoroughly, and then serve.

Easy Roasted Zucchini

Ingredients:

- 2 lbs. zucchini, (about 4 medium), trimmed and cut into ½inch slices

- 1 tbsp. extravirgin olive oil

Directions:

1. Set the oven with a baking tray on the middle rack. Preheat oven to 500 degrees F.
2. In a big bowl, toss zucchini with oil. Arrange a single layer of zucchini on the prepared baking tray. Roast 57 minutes until starting to brown. Turn zucchini and keep roasting 79 minute longer, until just tender.

Gomen

Ingredients:

- 2 tbsps. minced fresh garlic

- 1 medium tomato, very finely chopped (almost pureed)

- 1 medium jalapeño pepper, sliced

- 1 tbsp. tikur azmud (see Tip), ground, or 1 tsp. each ground cardamom and cumin

- 2 bunches collard greens (1½–1¾ lbs.), stemmed and finely chopped

- 1 cup minced red onion

- 2 tbsps. water

- ¼ cup extravirgin olive oil

- ¾ tsp. sea salt

Directions:

1. Bring water in a large pot to a boil over high heat. Add collards; cook for about 15 minutes until tender. Transfer to a colander to drain.
2. Cook onion and 2 tbsps. of water over medium heat in that pot for 4 to 5 minutes, stirring frequently, until onion is translucent.
3. Add garlic and oil; cook for another 1 minute, stirring well while cooking. Add jalapeno and tomato; cook for 5 minutes, stirring occasionally.
4. Mix in the greens; cook, covered, for 10 minutes, stirring once or twice.
5. Turn heat down to medium low. Mix in tikur azmud (or cumin and cardamom); cook, covered for 3 minutes longer. Turn off the heat. Mix in salt.

Instant Pot Butter Chicken

Ingredients:

- Ground turmeric ½ teaspoon
- Unsweetened tomato paste ½ cup
- Unsalted and unsweetened pure almond butter ½ cup
- Fullfat unsweetened coconut milk 15 ounces
- Arrowroot flour 1 tablespoon
- Water ¼ cup
- Cooked cauliflower rice 4 ounces
- Chopped parsley ¼ cup
- Olive oil 2 tablespoons
- Cubed b2 less skinless chicken breast 2 pounds

- Chopped white onion ½ cup

- Minced garlic 1 teaspoon

- Ginger 1 teaspoon

- Curry leaves 1 teaspoon

Directions:

1. Turn on the sauté setting in an Instant Pot. Heat the olive oil, then add the diced chicken and brown for 8 minutes, stirring occasionally.
2. Add onion, garlic and ginger. Stir well and cook for another 3 minutes. Press Cancel when d2 .
3. Add curry leaves, turmeric powder, tomato paste, almond butter and coconut milk. Lock the cover and close the valve. Cook on manual setting for 10 minutes. When the timer goes off, press "Quick Release".
4. In a small bowl, mix together the arrowroot flour and water.
5. Once all the pressure is released, remove the lid and press the sauté function. Gradually add the arrowroot pulp and stir for 12 minutes until the sauce thickens. Press Cancel.
6. Serve warm butter chicken over cauliflower rice garnished with fresh parsley.

Veggiepacked Turkey Meatloaf

Ingredients:

- Dried thyme 1 tsp.

- Dried oregano 1 tsp.

- Chopped spinach 4 ounces

- Chopped mushrooms ½ cup

- Chopped yellow onion ½ cup

- Chopped bell peppers ¾ cup

- Olive oil 1 tbsp.

- Ground almond ½ cup

- 2 whisked eggs

- Paleo ketchup ½ cup

- Black pepper ½ tsp.

- Fennel seeds ½ tsp.

- Onion powder 1 tsp.

- Dried basil 1 tsp.

- Red pepper flakes ½ teaspoon

- Ground turkey 2 pounds

Directions:

1. In a large bowl, combine the turkey, egg and ground almonds until well combined.
2. Heat the olive oil in a large skillet, then fry the bell peppers and onion for a few minutes until softened slightly.
3. Fry the mushrooms for a minute.
4. Fry the chopped spinach and cook until it starts to wilt. Turn off the heat.

5. Allow the vegetables to cool slightly, then add the vegetables and remaining seasonings (except the paleo ketchup) to the turkey. Mix with your hands, being careful not to over mix.
6. Pour the mixture evenly into a bread pan lined with parchment paper. Top with paleo ketchup.
7. Bake for an hour at 350°F, then cool for 10 minutes and serve sliced.

Golden Glow Soup

Ingredients:

- Fullfat coconut milk 1 cup

- Turmeric 1 teaspoon

- Coriander 1 teaspoon

- Ground ginger 1 teaspoon

- A pinch of cayenne pepper

- Chopped cabbage 2 cups

- Sesame seeds ¼ cup

- Olive oil 3 tablespoons

- Chopped carrots 2 cups

- 1 chopped and deseeded orange pepper

- 2 sliced chilies

- Paleo veggie broth 5 cups

- Fresh black pepper ½ teaspoon

Directions:
1. In a large skillet, heat 3 tablespoons of oil over medium heat, then fry the chopped carrots, orange pepper, and chili for about 10 minutes.
2. Add paleo veggie broth, coconut milk, and spices. Cover the skillet and simmer for about 1520 minutes.
3. Place the cabbage in a pot with 1 tablespoon of olive oil over medium heat. Cook, covered, for about five minutes, then set aside.
4. Once the soup is ready, puree the soup with a hand immersion blender until smooth.
5. Top the soup with the cabbage and sesame seeds. Serve hot!

Wholewheat Flatbreads With Beans & Poached Egg

Ingredients:

- 3 tsp smoked paprika

- 1 tsp balsamic vinegar

- 400g can haricot beans, drained

- For the flatbreads

- 100g wholewheat flour

- 2 eggs

- For the beans

- 500g carton passata

- 2 small onions, quartered

- 1 medjool date, st2 d

- ½ tsp baking powder, 100g natural yogurt

Directions:

1. Pour the passata into a food processor with the onions, date and paprika, and blend until it's completely smooth.
2. Heat the mixture in a medium pan, cover it and let it simmer for 10 minutes, stirring it often to make a thick, pulpy sauce.
3. Taste it to make sure the onion is cooked through; if not, add a splash of water and cook it a bit longer. Once it's d2 , stir in the vinegar and beans, then take it off the heat.
4. To make the flatbreads, mix the flour and baking powder in a bowl, then stir in the yogurt to make a soft dough.
5. Put it on a lightly floured surface and knead it, making sure to incorporate any flour left in the bowl.

6. Divide the dough in half and flatten each piece into a rough oval shape, using your hands or a rolling pin, until it's about the thickness of 3 £1 coins.
7. Cut slashes through the centre of the ovals a couple of times with a sharp knife, being careful not to cut through an edge.

Smoky Mushroom & Potato Hash With Oaty Thins

Ingredients:

- 100g of porridge oats

- 70 ml of fortified soya milk

- A half teaspoon of baking powder

- For the hash, you'll need 3 medium potatoes (275g) cut into slim wedges

- 3 tablespoons of rapeseed oil

- 160g of mushrooms, thickly sliced

- 2 red onion

- Roughly chopped

- 2 teaspoon of smoked paprika,

- 4 vine tomatoes halved 3 eggs.

Directions:

1. Mix the oats and soya milk in a large bowl and blend with a hand blender until the oats are less coarse.
2. Let it sit for 10 minutes. Boil the potatoes for 5 minutes, then drain. Heat some oil in a nonstick pan over medium heat and cook the mushrooms, onion, and paprika until softened.
3. Add the potatoes and cook for 10 minutes, stirring occasionally. Throw in the halved tomatoes and cook for another 5 minutes.
4. The oat mixture should now be thick. Incorporate the baking powder with your hands, then divide the mixture in half.
5. Wet your hands and press 2 half of the mixture on a plastic chopping board to make a thin disc, like a pancake.

6. Carefully lift it off with a palette knife and cook in a dry nonstick pan for 2 minutes on each side. Place it on a plate and repeat with the other half.
7. While the second 2 is cooking, push the potato mixture to the side in the other pan, crack in the eggs and cook until the whites are set and the yolks are still runny, about 23 minutes.
8. Serve the oat thins topped with the mushroom hash and eggs.

Pineapplecashew Soup

Ingredients:

- 2 tsp green Chili Paste
- ¼ tsp Clove Powder
- ¼ tsp Cinnamon Powder
- 1 tsp Sugar
- Salt to taste
- 2 cup ripe Pineapple (finely diced)
- 1 cup cashew nuts (grinded to a powder)
- 2 cups of Coconut Milk

Directions:

1. Steamcook the diced pineapple and add powdered cashew nuts to it.

2. Now blend this mixture into juice. (add 1 cup of water while blending)
3. Then add coconut milk, green chili paste, clove powder and cinnamon powder to the pineapplecashew juice. Mix it well and then bring it to a boil over medium heat.
4. Add salt and sugar as per taste and serve hot.

Green Peas – Carrot Soup

Ingredients:

- 1 tsp green Chili Paste

- 23 Neem Leaves

- ¼ tsp Cumin Seeds

- 2 Cloves

- Small Cinnamon stick

- 3 tsp Lemon Juice

- Salt to taste

- 1 cup Carrots (finely diced)

- ½ cup green peas

- 1 ½ cup Coconut Milk

- 12 tbsp Cooking Oil (Ghee i.e. clarified butter, Olive Oil, Avocado Oil or Coconut Oil)

Directions:
1. Mix diced carrot and green peas together, add 1 ½ cup of water to them and boil them till they are properly cooked, then set them aside.
2. Bring the coconut milk to a boil and add the boiled carrots and green peas to the coconut milk followed by green chili paste, salt and neem leaves.
3. Once the mixture boils properly, turn off the heat.
4. Heat the cooking oil in a pan.
5. Once the oil is hot, add the cumin seeds, cloves and cinnamon to the pan.
6. Once the cumin starts crackling, add the contents of the pan to the boiled soup mixture and mix well.

7. Before serving, heat up the soup a bit and add lemon juice.

Onion Soup

Ingredients:

- 1½ tsp Flour

- ¼ tsp black Pepper Powder

- 2 tsp grated Indian Cottage Cheese (Paneer)

- 1 tbsp chopped Coriander Leaves

- Salt to taste

- 1 medium sized Onion

- 2 tsp Butter

- 2 cups fresh Water

Directions:

1. Finely dice the onion.

2. Heat the butter in a pot and once the butter melts, add the diced onion and stir well till the onion turn light pink.
3. Then add the flour to the onions and stir well for a minute.
4. Then add water to the pot and bring it to a boil, all the while stirring constantly.
5. Then add salt and black pepper powder to the soup and stir for a couple of minutes.
6. Garnish with coriander leaves and serve hot.

AIP Lamb And Root Vegetable

Ingredients:

- 2 carrots, chopped

- 3 celery stalks, chopped

- 4 cloves garlic, crushed

- 1 teaspoon salt

- 1 teaspoon dried mint

- 34 lbs AIPcompliant lamb b2 s (shank or neck b2 s)

- 4 quarts water

- 2 tablespoons apple cider vinegar

- 1 onion, quartered

- 1 bay leaf

Directions:

1. Place lamb b2 s in a large stockpot.
2. Add water and apple cider vinegar. Let it sit for 30
1. minutes.
2. Add quartered onion, chopped carrots, celery, crushed garlic, salt, mint, and bay leaf.
3. Bring to a boil and then reduce heat to simmer.
4. Skim off any foam that rises to the top.
5. Simmer for 2448 hours, adding water as needed.
6. Strain the broth through a finemesh sieve or cheesecloth.
7. Cool and store in jars or containers. Refrigerate for up to a week or freeze for longer storage.

AIP Chicken And Vegetable Stew

Ingredients:

- 3 cloves garlic, minced

- 4 cups AIPcompliant chicken broth

- 1 cup chopped kale

- 1 teaspoon dried thyme

- Salt and pepper to taste

- 1.5 lbs AIPcompliant chicken thighs, b2 less and skinless, cut into chunks

- 2 sweet potatoes, peeled and diced

- 2 carrots, peeled and sliced

- 1 onion, chopped

- Fresh parsley for garnish (op onal)

Directions:

1. In a large pot, brown the chicken pieces over medium heat.
2. Add chopped onions and minced garlic, cooking un l so ened.
3. S r in sweet potatoes, carrots, chicken broth, and dried thyme.
4. Bring to a boil, then reduce heat and simmer for 45 minutes to 1 hour or un l vegetables are tender.
5. Add chopped kale and cook un l wilted.
6. Season with salt and pepper to taste.
7. Garnish with fresh parsley if desired. Serve and enjoy this comfor ng chicken and vegetable stew!

AIP Beef And Root Vegetable Stew

Ingredients:

- 4 cups AIPcompliant beef broth

- 2 cups diced bu ernut squash

- 2 tablespoons coconut oil

- 1 teaspoon dried rosemary

- Salt and pepper to taste

- 2 lbs AIPcompliant beef stew meat, cubed

- 3 parsnips, peeled and chopped

- 3 carrots, peeled and chopped

- 1 onion, chopped

- Fresh thyme for garnish (op onal)

Directions:

1. In a large pot, brown the beef cubes in coconut oil over medium heat.
2. Add chopped onions and cook un l translucent.
3. S r in parsnips, carrots, bu ernut squash, beef broth, and dried rosemary.
4. Bring to a boil, then reduce heat and simmer for 1.5
5. to 2 hours or un l the beef is tender.
6. Season with salt and pepper to taste.
7. Garnish with fresh thyme if desired. Serve and savor this hearty beef and root vegetable stew!

Zucchini Fritters With Avocado Dipping Sauce

Ingredients:

- 2 tablespoons chives

- 2 large eggs

- ½ teaspoon sea salt

- 3 tablespoons vegetable oil (for frying)

- 3 cups shredded zucchini

- ¼ cup allpurpose flour

- ¼ teaspoon garlic powder

- 2 tablespoons parmesan cheese

For the Avocado Dipping Sauce:

- ¼ cup Greek yogurt

- 1 garlic clove, finely minced

- ¼ teaspoon sea salt

- Pinch of freshly ground black pepper

- 2 avocados, peeled and pitted

- 2 tablespoons fresh lemon juice

Directions:

1. In a large bowl, combine the shredded zucchini, flour, garlic powder, parmesan cheese, and chives and stir until evenly combined.
2. In a small bowl, whisk together the eggs and salt. Pour the egg mixture into the zucchini mixture and stir until combined.
3. Heat the vegetable oil in a large skillet over mediumhigh heat. Once the oil is hot, spoon the mixture into the pan in small patties. Fry for 23 minutes on each side, or until golden brown.
4. Meanwhile, prepare the avocado dipping sauce. Mash the avocados in a separate bowl. Add the lemon juice, Greek yogurt, garlic, salt, and pepper and mix until combined.
5. Serve the zucchini fritters hot with the avocado dipping sauce.

Turkey And Sweet Potato Chili

Ingredients:

- 2 tablespoons chili powder

- 2 teaspoons ground cumin

- 2 (15ounce) cans kidney beans, rinsed and drained

- 1 (28ounce) can diced tomatoes

- 1 cup chicken broth

- 2 pounds ground turkey

- 1 large sweet potato, peeled and diced

- 1 onion, finely diced

- 2 cloves garlic, minced

- Optional toppings: shredded cheese, chopped green onions, diced avocado

Directions:

1. In a large pot over mediumhigh heat, cook the ground turkey until lightly browned.
2. Add the diced sweet potato, onion, garlic, chili powder, and cumin. Cook for 5 minutes, stirring occasionally.
3. Add the kidney beans, diced tomatoes, chicken broth, and stir.
4. Bring the mixture to a boil, then reduce the heat and simmer for 30 minutes or until the sweet potatoes are soft and the chili has thickened.
5. Serve warm with desired toppings.

Roasted Garlic And Herb Pork Tenderloin

Ingredients:

- 2 tbsp freshly chopped herbs (ie. rosemary, thyme, tarragon, etc.)

- 2 tbsp olive oil

- 1 lb pork tenderloin

- 2 cloves garlic, minced

- Salt and freshly ground black pepper to taste

Directions:
1. Preheat oven to 375° F
2. In a large bowl, marinate the pork with minced garlic, herbs, olive oil, salt and pepper for about 10 minutes.
3. Place pork in a shallow roasting pan and bake for 4045 minutes or until cooked through.
4. Let rest for 5 minutes before slicing.

Salmon Veggie Bowls With Sesame Seeds

Ingredients:

- 1/2 cup shredded green cabbage

- 2 tbsp avocado oil

- Sea salt and black pepper to taste

- A pinch dried thyme

- 1 lemon, juiced

- 1 tbsp olive oil

- 2 to 3 salmon fillets, cut into 1inch chunks

- Salt and black pepper to taste

- 4 cups green salad mix

- 1 tomato, deseeded and thinly sliced

- Sesame seeds to garnish

Directions:

1. Heat olive oil in skillet, season salmon with salt, black pepper, and cook in skillet until golden brown and flaky within, 3 minutes. Turn heat off and allow warming.
2. Combine remaining Ingredients: in a salad bowl except for sesame seeds.
3. Add salmon and mix well.
4. Serve.

Tilapia Veracruz

Ingredients:

- ½ cup unsweetened tomato sauce
- 3 garlic cloves, minced
- ½ cup pitted black olives, sliced
- 1 jalapeño pepper, chopped
- 1 tbsp capers, drained and rinsed
- 1 tbsp oregano
- 1 lemon, juiced
- 3 tbsp olive oil
- 1 medium onion, sliced
- 1 red bell pepper, sliced

- 2 tomatoes, chopped

- Kosher salt and black pepper, to taste

- 4 tilapia fillets

Directions:
1. Heat olive oil in a large skillet over medium heat.
2. Sauté onion, bell pepper, and tomatoes until softened, 5 minutes. Season with salt and black pepper.
3. Mix in remaining Ingredients: up to tilapia and slightly season with salt and black pepper.
4. Spice tilapia with salt, black pepper, and sit on sauce. Cover lid and cook over low heat for 5 to 6 minutes or until fish is flaky.
5. Dish fish with sauce, garnish with parsley and enjoy with mashed potatoes (dairyfree).

Shrimp And Sausage Skillet

Ingredients:

- 1 medium red bell pepper, seeded and chopped

- 2 garlic cloves, diced

- 1 zucchini, chopped

- 6 oz precooked smoked sausage, chopped

- ¼ cup homemade chicken stock

- Salt and black pepper to taste

- Pinch of red pepper flakes

- 1 tbsp coconut oil

- 1 lb jumbo shrimp, peeled and deveined

- 2 tsp Old Bay seasoning

- 1 small red onion, chopped

- 1 medium green bell pepper, seeded and chopped

- ½ medium yellow bell pepper, seeded and chopped

- Chopped fresh parsley to garnish

Directions:

1. Heat olive oil in large skillet over medium heat.
2. Season shrimp with Old Bay seasoning and cook in oil until opaque, 3 to 4 minutes. Transfer to a plate and set aside.
3. Cook onion, bell peppers, and garlic to skillet and cook until tender, 4 minutes.
4. Stir in zucchini, sausage and cook for 2 minutes.

5. Return shrimp to skillet, pour in chicken stock, and season with salt, black pepper, and red chili flakes. Stir until moistened and simmer for 1 minute.
6. Dish food and garnish with parsley. Serve warm.

Sweet Potato Hash Browns

Ingredients:

- 2 teaspoons sea salt

- 1/4 cup green onions, chopped (plus some for garnish)

- 1/4 cup coconut oil

- 4 medium sweet potatoes

- 2 eggs, whisked

- 1/2 cup almond flour

Directions:

1. Puncture 2 of the sweet potatoes with a fork. Wrap it in a moist paper towel and place it in a little bowl with 1/2 inch of water. Microwave for 79 minutes, or until delicate.

2. Give this sweet potato a chance to sit for 5 minutes. At that point deplete the water, peel the potato, and squash it with a fork.
3. Take the other 3 sweet potatoes and peel them. At that point grate them on a crate grater utilizing the expansive openings. In your dish of ground sweet potatoes, include the past pounded potato, the 2 eggs, almond flour, ocean salt, and green onion. Join with a spoon.
4. In a skillet (I utilized cast iron), pour coconut oil and warmth over medium until your cast iron is hot. In the event that you have a thermometer, it ought to peruse 350 degrees. At that point drop in sweet potato "cakes" in around 23 tablespoon clumps. Level them with a spatula. Cook on every side for 5 minutes or until brilliant chestnut.
5. Once cooked, place on a plate with paper towels to deplete the oil. Serve hot.

Turkey Sausage Breakfast

Ingredients:

- 2 tsp. Sea Salt

- 2 Tbsp. Mary's G2 Crackers, crushed

- 1 egg, lightly beaten

- 2 Tbsp. ghee

- 1 lb. ground or shredded turkey

- 1/2 small onion, finely diced

- 1/4 tsp. each: Cumin, marjoram, Black Pepper, Oregano, Cayenne Pepper, Ginger

- 1/2. tsp. each: Basil, Thyme, sage

Directions:

1. Sauté onions in 1 Tbsp. Butter until soft and translucent.
2. Combine all Ingredients: (except remaining butter) in a large bowl
3. Form into patties and cook in remaining butter

Turkey, Bacon Lettuce Wraps With Basil And Mayonnaise

Ingredients:

- 4 slices glutenfree bacon, cooked (I like Applegate Farms)

- 1 avocado, thinly sliced

- 1 roma tomato, thinly sliced

- 1 head iceberg lettuce

- 4 slices glutenfree deli turkey (I like Applegate Farms)

For the basilmayonnaise:

- 6 large basil leaves, torn

- 1 teaspoon lemon juice

- 1 garlic clove, chopped

- 1/2 cup glutenfree mayonnaise (I like Hellmann's Olive Oil Mayo)

- salt

- pepper

Directions:

1. For the BasilMayonnaise: consolidate fixings in a little sustenance processor then process until smooth.
2. On the other hand, mince basil and garlic then whisk all fixings together. Should be possible a few days early.
3. Lay out 3 substantial lettuce leaves then layer on 1 cut of turkey and slather with BasilMayo.
4. Layer on a second cut of turkey took after by the bacon, and a couple cuts of both avocado and tomato.
5. Season daintily with salt and pepper then overlap the base up, the sides in, and move

like a burrito. Cut down the middle then serve chilly.

Chop & Drop Roasted Veggies & Sausage

Ingredients:

- 1 red pepper, cut into large slices

- 1/2 red onion, peeled and cut into large slices

- 3 cloves of minced or pressed garlic

- 2 tbs of olive oil

- 1 1/2 tbs of Italian seasoning

- A healthy pinch of red pepper flakes

- Salt & pepper to taste

- 1 package (or about 1 lb) of your favorite precooked sausage links – cut into 1inch long sections (In this case I used Applegate brand)

- 2 potatoes (1 yam and 1 white flesh sweet potato) cut into 2inch chunks

- 2 mediumsize carrots, chopped into small rounds

- Plus any additional seasonings you desire

Directions:
1. Preheat oven to 375degrees F
2. In a large mixing bowl, add all sliced veggies, garlic and cut sausage links
3. Next add olive oil and toss everything to coat
4. Sprinkle in all seasonings and mix again to distribute
5. Now grease or line with aluminum foil a largerimmed baking sheet
6. Spread out the veggies and sausage across the baking sheet
7. Place uncovered in oven

8. Bake a total of 35 to 45 minutes, turning veggies and sausage twice during cooking. (Oven temperatures and times will vary)
9. Test d2 ness by checking the sweet potatoes – if they're soft, it's d2
10. Serve hot and enjoy!

Portobello Burgers

Ingredients:

For the hamburgers

- 3 eggs

- 2 cloves garlic, minced

- Sea salt and freshly ground black pepper to taste

- Makes 6 to 8 patties

- 3lbs of ground beef (not too lean if you want a very flavorful patty)

For the portobello mushrooms

- 68 large Portabello mushrooms

- A few tablespoons of olive oil (the amount will depend on how large your mushrooms are, so start with a little and add more as needed)

- 2 cloves garlic, minced

- Sea salt and freshly ground black pepper to taste

Directions:

For the hamburgers

1. Place the ground beef in a large bowl and add the eggs. Combine until the eggs are evenly mixed through.
2. Mix in the garlic and season with salt and pepper.
3. Form 6 to 8 patties that are slightly smaller than the mushroom caps so they can fit on top once cooked.Place on a preheated grill and cook each side for about 57 minutes (the time it takes will depend on the temperature

of your grill. I cooked them at mediumlow for approximately this time).

For the portobello mushrooms

4. Rinse the mushrooms and pat them dry.
5. Remove the mushroom stems. The reason for this is because you want your mushroom cap to take the form of the hamburger bun. Do not discard, they can be great for many other recipes, or you can grill them along with the caps.
6. Coat the caps in olive oil and then season with salt and pepper. Do not let the oil penetrate for long, as you will notice the mushrooms will start to get soggy.
7. Place on the preheated grill and cook on each side for about 57 minutes.
8. Now all there is left to do is stack your patty on top of your mushroom and add any toppings you desire.

Chicken And Sweet Potato Skillet

Ingredients:

- Onion, chopped

- Garlic, minced

- Coconut oil

- Chicken breasts, cubed

- Sweet potatoes, peeled and diced

- Salt and pepper to taste

Directions:

1. In a skillet, heat coconut oil over medium heat.
2. Add chicken and cook until browned. Remove from the skillet.

3. In the same skillet, sauté onions and garlic until softened.
4. Add sweet potatoes and cook until tender.
5. Return the cooked chicken to the skillet. Season with salt and pepper.

Sesame Steak And Vegetable Stir Fry

Ingredients:

- 1 cup chopped broccoli

- 1 cup green beans, trimmed

- 1 1/2 tablespoons sesame seeds

- 2 1/2 tablespoons green onions chopped

- 2 tablespoons coconut aminos

- 2 tablespoons warm water

- 3/4 tsp ginger

- 1 1/2 pound lean sirloin steak

- 3/4 cup red bell pepper, julienned

- 3/4 cup red onion, julienned

- 1 tablespoon coconut oil

- 1 tablespoon minced garlic

Directions:

1. In a skillet on mediumhigh, add oil, and place the steak which has been cut into 1/4 inch strips. Sauté the steak till cooked through, and remove and place on the serving plate.
2. Add the onion, broccoli, green beans, and sauté for 5 min. In a bowl combine the coconut aminos, water, garlic, and ginger. Whisk these together till smooth.
3. Add the meat and sauce to the pan with the vegetables, and toss lightly, heat for 5 min.
4. Toss the stir fry with the green onions and the sesame seeds. Makes 4 servings.

Baked Salmon With Lemon And Pecan Green Beans

Ingredients:

- 1 tablespoon thyme

- 1 tablespoon capers

- 2 tablespoons lemon juice

- 2 tablespoons extra virgin olive oil

- 4 (8 ounce) pieces of salmon

- Unrefined sea salt and pepper to taste

Directions:

1. Prepare to line a rimmed baking sheet with parchment paper and place salmon skin side down on the baking sheet. Season it with sea salt and pepper. Spoon the lemon juices on

the salmon, place the capers, and drizzle the oil on top.

2. Bake at 400° for 30 min. Makes 4 servings.

Butter Chicken

Ingredients:

- 2 tsp garam masala

- 1 tsp curry powder

- 1/2 tsp ground ginger

- 1/2 tsp chili powder, add more if you like it hotter

- 1 pinch sea salt

- 1 pinch black pepper

- 1 tbsp organic coconut oil

- 3 4 whole garlic, crushed

- 1 whole onion, diced

- 1 3/4 cup coconut milk

- 3/4 cup tomato paste

- 2 tbsp arrowroot flour

- 2 1/5 lb skinless chicken breast

Directions:

1. Heat coconut oil in a large saucepan on medium high heat.
2. Add onion and garlic, cook, stirring frequently for approximately 3 minutes or until the onions have become translucent.
3. Add coconut milk, tomato paste, tapioca flour, garam masala, curry powder, ginger powder, chili powder and ginger powder, stirring until well combined and the sauce has started to thicken.
4. Season with salt and pepper.

5. Add chicken to the slow cooker, then add the sauce and mix through the chicken.
6. Cover and cook on low heat for 5 hours.Cover and cook on low heat for 5 hours.
7. Serve with coriander and your favourite side.

Slow Cooker Ham

Ingredients:

- 2 tsp Dried Rosemary

- 4 tbs Coconut Oil

- Zest of 1 Orange

- 1 46 lb Ham Roast

- 1/4 cup H2 y

- 1/2 cup Orange Juice

- 1 tbs Apple Cider Vinegar

Directions:
1. Place ham in slow cooker.
2. Put the rest of the Ingredients: on the ham.
3. Cook on low for 46 hours.

Pumpkin Slow Cooker Coconut Curry

Ingredients:

- 2 teaspoon garam masala

- 1/2 teaspoon Kosher salt

- 1/4 teaspoon ground black pepper

- 1/2 large onion, diced

- 1 garlic clove, minced

- 3 carrots, cut into 1inch pieces

- 3 cups 1inch cubed sweet potatoes

- 2 chicken breasts, cut into 1inch cubes

- Juice of 1 lime

- 1 15ounce can of unsweetened coconut milk (full fat, not light)

- 2 cups pumpkin puree (not pumpkin pie filling)

- 1 cup chicken stock

- 1/2 tablespoon curry powder

- 1/4 teaspoon tumeric powder

Directions:
1. In the insert of a 4quart or larger slow cooker, add the coconut milk, pumpkin puree, chicken stock, curry powder, tumeric powder, garam masala, salt, and pepper.
2. Whisk together to make sure it is all combined and spices are evenly distributed.

3. Add the onion, garlic, carrots, sweet potatoes, chicken breasts, and lime juice to the mixture. Stir to coat and incorporate.
4. Cook on low for 6 hours.
5. Serve over rice.

Vegetable Broth

Ingredients:

- 8 sprigs fresh parsley

- 6 sprigs fresh thyme

- 2 bay leaves

- 1 tsp. salt

- 2 quarts water

- 1 tbsp. coconut oil

- 1 large onion

- 2 stalks celery, including some leaves

- 2 large carrots

- 1 bunch green onions, chopped

- 8 cloves garlic, minced

Directions:

1. Chop veggies into small chunks. Heat oil in a soup pot and add onion, scallions, celery, carrots, garlic, parsley, thyme, and bay leaves. Cook over high heat for 5 to 7 minutes, stirring occasionally.
2. Bring to a boil and add salt. Lower heat and simmer, uncovered, for 30 minutes. Strain. Other Ingredients: to consider: broccoli stalk, celery root

Curry Paste

Ingredients:

- 2 (2 inch) pieces cinnamon sticks, crushed
- 1 tsp. ground cumin
- 1 tsp. ground coriander
- 1 tsp. salt
- 1 tsp. ground cayenne pepper
- 1 tsp. ground turmeric
- 2 onions, minced
- 2 cloves garlic, minced
- 2 teaspoons fresh ginger root, finely chopped
- 6 whole cloves
- 2 cardamom pods

Directions:

1. Heat oil in a frying pan over medium heat and fry onions until transparent. Stir in garlic, cumin, ginger, cloves, cinnamon, coriander, salt, cayenne, and turmeric.
2. Cook for 1 minute over medium heat, stirring constantly. At this point other curry Ingredients: should be added.

Frittata

Ingredients:

- Crispy bacon, 3 slices

- Chopped kale, destemmed and rinsed 2 cups

- Eggs 8

- Almond or coconut milk ½ cup

- Coconut oil 1 tbsp.

- Finely chopped red pepper ½ cup

- Finely diced onion 1/3 cup

- Salt and pepper to taste

Directions:

1. Preheat oven to 350 degrees F. Whisk the eggs and milk together. Season with salt and pepper. Keep it aside for the time being.
2. Heat a skillet and add the coconut oil. Once the oil is hot, sauté the pepper and onion until soft. Add kale and cook till it wilts. This whole process takes about 5 minutes.
3. To the above mixture add the bacon and the eggs and cook till the frittata sets.
4. Put this frittata in the preheated oven and cook for 1015 minutes or until it is fully cooked. Take it out. Slice it and serve.

No Flour No Sugar Paleo Brownie

Ingredients:

- Almond butter 1 cup
- Maple syrup 1/3 cup
- Egg 1
- Ghee 2 tbsp.
- Vanilla 1 tsp
- Cocoa powder 1/3 cup
- Baking soda ½ tsp

Directions:

1. Preheat the oven to 325°F. In a large bowl, whisk together the almond butter, maple

syrup, egg, ghee, and vanilla. Stir in the cocoa powder and baking soda.
2. Pour the batter into a 9inch baking pan. Bake for 2023 minutes, until the brownie is d2 , but still soft in the middle.

Dark Chocolate Mousse

Ingredients:

- 1/2 cup organic cacao powder

- 1 tsp instant coffee

- 1/4 tsp Ancho Chili powder

- 1/4 tsp Himalayan salt

- 1 ripe avocado

- 1/4 cup date paste

- 1 tbsp. unpasteurized h2 y

- 1 cup full fat coconut milk

- 1 tbsp. pure vanilla extract

Directions:

1. Puree the dates paste, avocado, h2 y and coconut milk until it turns into a smooth paste.
2. To this puree add the cacao powder, coffee, chili powder, salt and vanilla and continue to blend till all the powders are nicely incorporated into the mixture.
3. Next whisk this entire mixture into a fluffy consistency either using a hand whisk or a stand mixer.
4. Your chocolate mousse is ready to be refrigerated. Transfer the mousse to individual bowls and refrigerate for 46 hours at least.
5. Though this mousse can be had straight away the taste is enhanced when had cold.
6. The above recipes will help you host your friends and family to a Paleo day wherein you can start with the breakfast and end with the dessert – all Paleo.

7. They will sure be surprised with the palatability and the great taste of Paleo food.

Quick And Easy Garlic Shrimp

Ingredients:

- 1/2 tsp fresh lemon juice
- 4 garlic cloves, minced
- 1/4 tsp sea salt
- 1/4 tsp ground black better
- 2 tbsp olive oil
- 1/2 tsp fresh lime juice
- 1 lb. large wildcaught shrimp, shelled and deveined

Directions:

1. Preheat oven broiler on high.

2. In a large bowl, add olive oil, fresh lime juice, lemon juice, garlic cloves, salt, and pepper. Whisk lightly to combine.
3. Add the shelled and deveined shrimp. Toss lightly to coat.
4. Spread shrimp evenly on an ovenproof baking pan.
5. Place in oven and broil for 3 minutes or until pink. Serve immediately.

Lamb And Cilantro Stir Fry

Ingredients:

- Juice of 1 lime

- 1/2 tsp coriander

- 1/2 tsp sea salt

- 1/2 tsp fresh ground pepper

- 1 bunch cilantro, chopped lightly

- 2 tbsp oil of choice

- 1 lb. b2 less lamb, cubed

- 1 clove garlic, minced

- 1 clove ginger, minced

- 1 red bell pepper, chopped

- 1 zucchini, sliced

Directions:

1. Heat oil in a large skillet or pan on mediumhigh heat. Add the lamb and cook until browned. Remove lamb and set aside.
2. Add garlic, ginger, red bell pepper, and zucchini into the pan. Cook until softened.
3. Add lime juice, coriander, salt and pepper. Add the lamb back to the pan and mix to combine.
4. Continue cooking until lamb is d2 . Sprinkle with chopped cilantro and serve.

Beef Stirfry

Ingredients:

- 3 cups mushrooms, quartered

- ½ head bok choy

- 1 1/2 lbs. top sirloin or flank steak, thinly sliced into strips

- 1 tablespoon minced garlic

- Coconut oil

Sauce:

- 2 tablespoons h2 y

- ½ cup gluten free soy sauce (tamari sauce)

- 2 tablespoons arrowroot powder

- 1 teaspoon ground ginger

Beef marinade:

- Freshly ground black pepper

- 1 1/2 teaspoons arrowroot powder

- 1 tablespoon gluten free soy sauce

Directions:

1. Slice beef into strips and place the strips in a large bowl. Combine the marinade Ingredients:, apply to the beef and then let the beef marinade for 1060 minutes.
2. In the meantime, slice the bok choy. Don't forget to remove the end of the stem.
3. In a small bowl, combine the sauce Ingredients: and set aside.
4. Heat coconut oil in skillet over medium heat. Brown the beef for 12 minutes on both sides. You can brown in batches to prevent overcrowding. Remove meat and set aside.
5. Add garlic, bok choy and mushrooms to the skillet and cook until tender before adding back the meat. Add sauce and cook for 23 more minutes to allow the sauce to thicken.
6. Remove and serve with cauliflower rice.

Cauliflower Rice

Ingredients:

- 1 large head cauliflower, trimmed and coarsely chopped
- 4 stalks celery, finely chopped
- 1 medium onion, finely chopped
- ¼ teaspoon sea salt
- 3 tablespoons olive oil

Directions:

1. Heat skillet over medium heat, add olive oil and then add onion and cook for 8-10 minutes or until soft. Add celery and continue cooking for 5 more minutes.
2. Pulse cauliflower in the food processor. It should resemble the texture of rice.

3. Place the cauliflower in skillet, cover the skillet and cook for 1520 minutes. Stir from time to time until soft.

Stirfry

Ingredients:

- ½ teaspoon sea salt

- 1 small zucchini, sliced

- 4 ounces shiitake mushrooms, stemmed and thinly sliced

- 2 heads baby bok choy, sliced crosswise into 1inch strips

- 2 medium carrots, sliced

- 2 heads broccoli, sliced into 3 inch spears

- 1 medium onion, finely chopped

- 2 tablespoons coconut oil

- 1 tablespoon h2 y

- 2 tablespoons vinegar

- 2 tablespoons toasted sesame oil

- 2 tablespoons arrowroot powder

- 11/2 cups water

- 1 pound b2 less, skinless chicken breast

Directions:
1. Rinse chicken and gently pat it dry before cutting into 1inch cubes; set aside on a plate.
2. Heat a large skillet over medium heat and add coconut oil. Add onion and cook for 810 minutes.
3. Add bok choy, zucchini, mushrooms and salt and cook for 5 more minutes. Add 1 cup of water, cover and cook for 10 minutes.
4. In a bowl, mix together ½ cup water and arrowroot powder. Pour the mixture over the vegetables and stir continuously for 23

minutes. Add vinegar, sesame oil and h2 y and stir to mix.
5. Serve and enjoy.

Creamy Dill Garlic Salmon

Ingredients:

- 2 teaspoons of brown mustard

- 1 clove of garlic (minced)

- Pinch of sea salt

- 2 salmon fillets (b2 s removed)

- 1/2 cup of mayonnaise

- 2 tablespoons of fresh dill (chopped)

Directions:
1. Preheat oven to 450 degrees.
2. Line a baking sheet with parchment paper.
3. Place the salmon fillets (skin side down) on the parchment paper.
4. Mix together the dill, mustard, garlic, salt, and mayonnaise.

5. Spread the mixture evenly over the salmon. Bake for about 810 minutes or until the fish begins to flake with a fork.
6. Serve hot and squeeze on lemon juice for flavor.

Bang Bang Shrimp

Ingredients:

- 3 tablespoons of coconut oil

- 1/2 cup of mayo

- 1 lb. of shrimp

- 1/2 cup of tapioca flour

- Sriracha for spice

Directions:

1. Heat the coconut oil in a skillet over a medium to medium high heat.
2. Coat each of the shrimp in the tapioca flour.
3. Fry each shrimp in the skillet until they are crispy on each side.
4. In a separate mixing bowl, mix together the mayo and Sriracha.

5. Toss the shrimp and Sriracha together.

   Homemade Cilantro Lime Ranch Dressing

Ingredients:

- 1/3 cup of milk (substitute for almond or coconut milk)

- 1/3 cup of cilantro (chopped)

- 2 tablespoons fresh chives (chopped)

- 23 cloves of garlic (minced)

- 1/4 teaspoon of salt

- 3/4 cup light mayo

- 3/4 cup greek yogurt

- 2 tablespoons of lime (juiced)

- 1 tablespoon of olive oil

- 1/4 teaspoon of black pepper

Directions:

1. Place all the Ingredients: into a blender.
2. Blend until smooth and creamy

Grilled Lemonherb Chicken

Ingredients:

- 2 tsps. snipped fresh thyme

- 1 tsp. snipped fresh rosemary

- ¼ tsp. crushed red pepper

- ¼ tsp. salt

- ⅛ tsp. ground black pepper

- Fresh thyme sprigs (optional)

- 6 b2 less chicken breast halves (about 1½ lbs. total)

- ¼ cup olive oil

- 6 cloves garlic, minced

- 1 tbsp. lemon peel, finely shredded

- Lemon wedges (optional)

Directions:

1. Transfer the chicken to a resealable plastic bag and set in a shallow bowl. For the marinade, mix oil, crushed red pepper, garlic, black pepper, lemon peel, rosemary, salt and thyme in a small bowl.
2. Spread the marinade atop chicken. Seal the bag and flip to coat the chicken. Place in a fridge to marinate for about 2 to 4 hours and turn the bag often.
3. Drain the chicken and get rid of the marinade.
4. Transfer the chicken onto the rack of an uncovered grill directly atop medium coals.
5. Let it grill for about 12 to 15 minutes or until no pink color of chicken remains, flipping once halfway through grilling (165 degrees F). Stud

with lemon wedges and fresh thyme sprigs if desired.

Maplechili Roasted Butternut Squash

Ingredients:

- 13 tsps. chili powder
- ½ tsp. salt
- 4 cups cubed butternut squash
- 4 small shallots, quartered
- 2 tbsps. pure maple syrup
- 2 tbsps. melted butter
- 1½ tsps. balsamic vinegar

Directions:

1. Preheat an oven to 425°F. With cooking spray, grease a big rimmed baking sheet.

2. In a big bowl, combine salt, chili powder, butter and maple syrup. Put in shallots and squash and equally coat by tossing.
3. On the prepped baking sheet, set in 1 layer.
4. Let the vegetables roast for 25 to 30 minutes, mixing 2 or 3 times, till soft. Sprinkle with vinegar prior to serving.

www.ingramcontent.com/pod-product-compliance
Lightning Source LLC
LaVergne TN
LVHW010224070526
838199LV00062B/4716